Kulture 4 Kids

Alex Bruno

A book by ALEX BRUNO
Edited by Anaya Bruno
With Preface by Noreen Joseph and Illustrations by Media Max.

First Edition

ISBN: 978-0-9915728-4-7

Typesetting G & D Enterprises Inc

The Lost-generation Heritage Series (L-GHS)
Book 2
About the Lost Generation

The lost generation, in this book, represents a predominant Caribbean mindset which is mainly demonstrated by individuals who had not made the shift to the cultural trends of the times, instead they hold on to traditions with the misguided notion that by so doing, they are indeed embracing and celebrating their culture. The issue is, however, that tradition is not culture and vice versa, so that prevailing attitude keeps those who subscribe to it caught-up in a sort of false Caribbean limbo.

This Caribbean limbo is found in the lost generation's attitude towards politics, spirituality and religion, culture and traditions, other traditions and global issues, development, customs, interpretations, conceptions of leadership, responses to leadership, the attitude towards past and emerging generations, and, most importantly, creating a stalemate in the link of progress from one era of Caribbean reality to another.

Examples of people who inhibit the traits of the lost generation would be the appreciation of one type of music Cadence, in the Dominican context. This view expresses a standard benchmark for that music as being a particular rhythmic pattern which does not, or should not evolve.

Those from the lost generation are slow in adapting to new and creative ways of cultural evolutions, they harbor a quasi-colonial mindset when it comes to practices and traditions, they maintain a sort of a mental block towards differing attitudes and ideas of Caribbeaness and progress, and they display disdain for challenges to their Caribbean disposition.

In my view, the lost generation is a Caribbean phenomenon. This is the case because the lack of indigenous construction, or founding, of the region. The lost generation generally encapsulates people between the age group of 36 - 56. People in that age bracket were born into a region, in the late 60s to mid-late 80s which was characterized by an attitude of reform and resistance. Those who reformed did a bit better than those who resisted. Resistance here means an anti-reformist attitude, and not resistance in the sense of pushing back against artificial notions of who we are as Caribbean people. In other words, the term 'lost generation' describe those who have/did not truly appreciate what the Caribbean is or was, or what it can become.

This L-GHS, which comprises of 4 separate books (Kaiso 4 Kids, Kadanse 4 Kids, Kwéyòl 4 Kids, Kulture 4 Kids) serves as a necessary spark of awareness. I believe it will assist in provoking the children to think beyond that lost generation gap in our Caribbean consciousness. These books are not just for Caribbean audiences; they are meant to embrace global attitudes of Caribbean traditions and culture, and to connect Caribbean children with others of different regions.

Alex Bruno

Preface

Welcome to Kulture 4 Kids, a delightful journey into the vibrant and diverse world of cultures from around the world.

This book is designed to enlighten young minds to appreciate the richness and beauty of cultural diversity, understanding and appreciation for many ways people live, celebrate and express themselves.

Today more than ever, it is important for everyone, especially children, to learn about different and various cultures, through the colourful stories and illustrations as you turn the pages of this book that Alex Bruno has written for you.

Whether you are reading alone, or with family and friends, Kulture 4 Kids promises to be an exciting and educational experience.

Join Alex Bruno on this journey as we learn about many rich and vibrant cultures that make our universe so colourful and interesting. Let us dive in and discover the beauty and wonder of culture, come let us explore this wonderful story together.

Noreen I Joseph
Dip. Education /BA Cultural studies (Theatre)

Introduction

Because of the intricate nature of the concepts which are covered in this book, we made the decision to present the text as a glossary, instead of a narrative discussion. I remember my days as a school boy when Sir Clarence Signoret - deceased former President of Dominica - visited my primary school at Calibishie and shook every student's hands.

I was among those students who received a brisk, firm handshake and a deep gaze in the eyes from Sir Clarence. Later in life, I invited Sir Clarence to speak with boys and girls who attended Reality Camp,
1992 - an event which I produced for boys and girls from the ages of 9 to teenhood. This was an amazing event where Sir Clarence took the time to teach us a lot about etiquette, protocol, discipline and the benefits of public service.

I later interviewed Sir Clarence on radio and he passed on the same good old teaching of etiquette, symbols of state, protocol, and public service. Therefore, most - if not all - of what is written in this book comes from the very rich bureaucratic awareness reservoir of Sir Clarence Signoret. In fact, this book is being presented in his honor. Michele Henderson is highlighted in this publication.

I hope that this small effort enables emerging generations to confront the otherwise difficult to grasp concepts and place them in their proper contexts when referring to civility and societies.

Prunella's disillusionment with culture began when her grandmother, Ms. Fejèni, scolded her severely for dancing hip-hop. The story is told that Prunella was dancing with her friends on the four roads when Ms. Fejèni pounced on her and said 'How dare you, Prunella, how dare you'.

Now, I am not sure whether this really happened in that particular way, but that was the talk in the village for weeks. Prunella herself told me that since then, she has not danced hip-hop, and she does not intend to anymore.

Prunella told me that grandma Fejèni told her that we needed to preserve our culture, and that by practicing other cultural forms, we were only watering down our own culture while promoting other peoples' culture.

I am only relating what was related to me, so, please do not hold me responsible for what I am saying. By the way, my name is Elias, and I do not agree with Ms. Fejèni. I may have lost my dancing skills due to age, but I still feel like a child.

There is a little child trapped in all of us, and my little child in me tells me that there is nothing wrong for Prunella to dance hip-hop.

If Prunella was with me now, I would have told her how I felt, but let me use this medium to try and connect with all the little Prunellas who might have been told similar.

I love to read, and write, so all of what I am about to share comes from what I have read; some are my own interpretation. I believe, as well, that some people seems to mix-up the terms, so I will attempt to treat each concept as its own unit of analysis in my own way.

Before I explain the 'concepts', I guess I must explain the term concept. I should explain 'unit of analyses as well of course.

Okay, a concept is the understanding of something in the mind. That something does not really have a singular identity, but there is a notion of realness to its abstract characteristic.

That is what concept is in a nutshell.

'Unit of analysis' means the particulars of that thing which is being analyzed. So, Citizenship, Colonialism, Creoles, Creole, Croelité, Culture, Folklore, Heritage, Identity, Nationhood and Tradition are all units which need their own separate analysis and contextual usages.

I am aware that I am introducing you to some new words, and concepts, but it will benefit you in the future. In any case, you could ask a family member, teacher, or any other knowledgeable person to help you with this book.

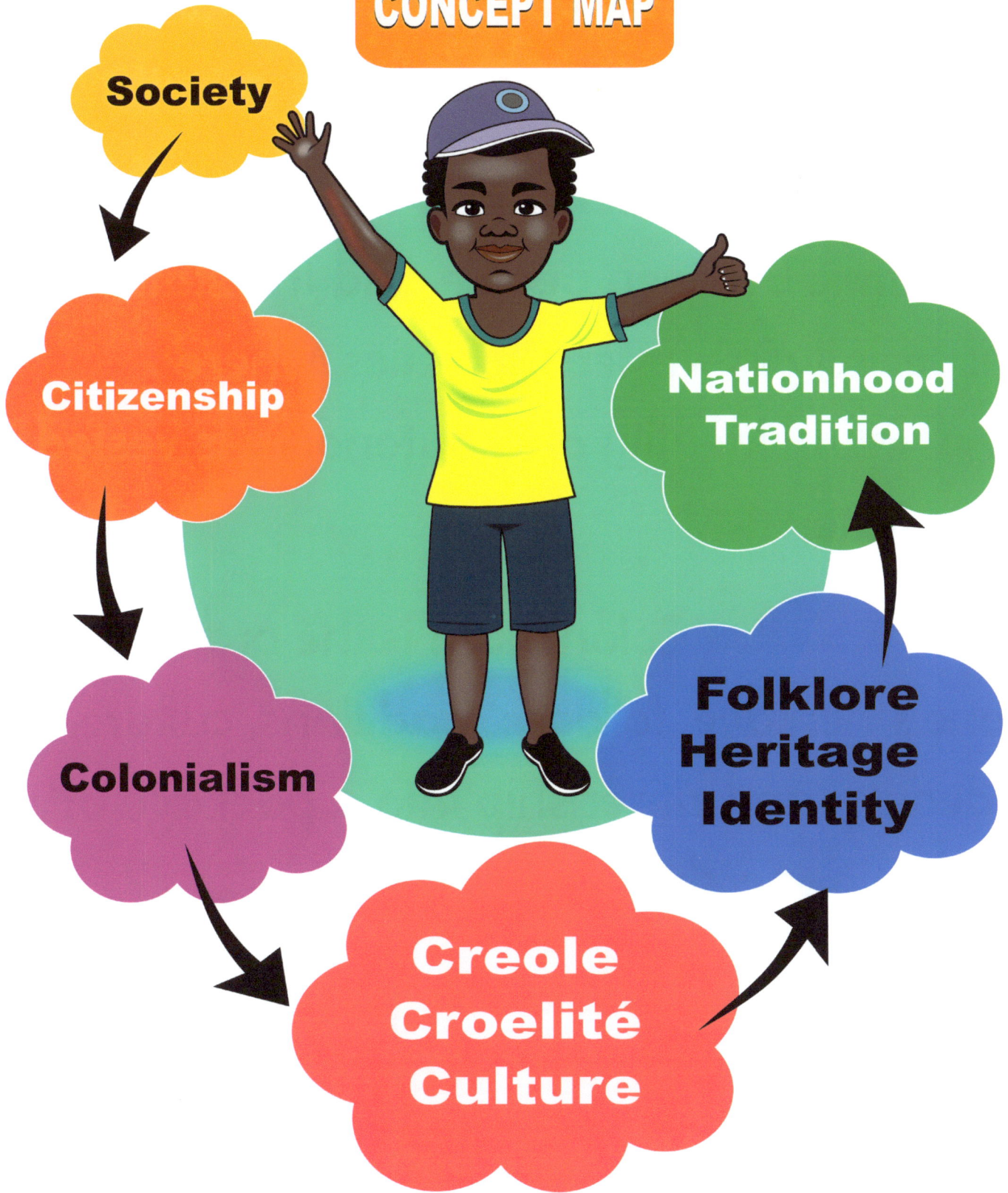

CONCEPT MAP

Society

Citizenship

Colonialism

Nationhood Tradition

Folklore Heritage Identity

Creole Croelité Culture

9

Let me now introduce you to the concepts which should help you to better relate to others in society in general. I begin with:

Citizenship: - Citizenship is an ever-changing dynamic between people and the state, especially in western societies, where individual identity and autonomy is vested in the state;

Colonialism: - Colonialism is the ordering of one's heritage, folklore, traditions, culture, identity, and citizenship into a package of rights, ownership and authority;

Creoles: - Creoles is a category of people who were either transplanted from the African mainland and/or were born within the colonial spaces.

So, not only 'Blacks' are Creoles, but there are 'White' Creoles, and Creoles of all ethnicities, cultures, traditions and origins as well;

a. It is true, as well, that the Creole attitude, including the linguistic forms, was developed by the displaced African, who skillfully synthesized many African Creole languages and modes of expression into one.

b. The spoken idiom known as Creole is, therefore, a hybrid and highly advanced manner of oral expression like no other. In fact, Creole is more than the spoken word; Creole is a general attitude of communication which can transcend words.

More precisely, Creole is a created category which denotes peoples of a particular birthright, or who exist within a specific birthplace, and Creoles is the sum of experiences of the creole peoples;

Creolité: - Creolité is an attitude of creoleness that transcends the bounds of colonial control;

Culture: - Culture is what emerges from who we are and the experiences of becoming;

Folklore: - Folklore is the seeds of traditions which grew out of people's thinking of their being;

Heritage: - Heritage is the idea of inheritance and how this informs the individuals' awareness of self;

Identity: - Identity is the placement of someone or a group in the wider sea of cultures;

Nationhood: - Nationhood or nationality is an expressed form of citizenship which rubs citizens from their agency in the interest of state autonomy;

Tradition: - The practice of one's heritage.

Here is how I would use all the concepts in one run-on phrase:

Society is comprised of people with varied Citizenship which are influenced by Colonialism; the global concept which created Creoles and a collective of individuals under the Creole banner who are connected by the distinct Croelité; the bedrock of their Culture.

This means that ideas like Folklore, Heritage and Identity are carefully weaved into one's Nationhood, and in fact, it is Tradition which has given definition to the modern.

In other words, what is now modern was once tradition, and today's modern will be tomorrow's tradition.

Okay, this was a mouthful, and I get the feeling that your mind is in active mode after reading this book. If it is, that is good because this is what was expected.

Now, here is what I would like you to do: maintain your childhood curiosity as an education endowment. Education is learning and teaching and endowment means quality or characteristic.

When we stop being curious, we begin to lose the essence of our very existence.

THE END

Recognizing Michele Henderson

I believe in appreciating people for what they have done and celebrating their achievements with the world. Generanations of Dominican and Caribbean women have represented the region's culture through music, culture, the performing and fine arts. Michele Henderson is one of them.

Michele is also an entrepreneur, voice coach, lyricist, literary artist, musician, an accomplished world-class multi-instrumentalist, recording artist, headliner, she is a musical arranger composer/producer and, and music business executive. Michele is an academic, intellectual properties expert, a mentor, and award-winning achiever who transcends all boarders.

The spotlight is therefore beamed of the Dominica songbird with the hope that her efforts be noted and preserved for posterity. Michele, however, would not agree that she is a stand-alone achiever.

Indee, she rides on a rich cultural tradition of high female achievers. Michele is a link in the unbroken chain of practitioners who have transcended gender and broken barriers. Michele represents a force for good and progress in our and for all times.

It is important to connect the dots of progress, and this books, in its own little way, present a platform for all the younger Michele's which exists in readers and reviewers of Kulture 4 Kids.

With the understanding that culture is continuum, it is hoped that the works of past greats continue to flourish through the current generations and that the future will be informed by that continuing tradition.

We are pleased to present Michele Henderson as the featured personality of the second book in the series – Kulture 4 Kids. May her work continue to inspire people the world over

About the Author

Alex Bruno has a vast array of accomplishments which complement his natural abilities and acquired skills. In addition to his experience as a broadcaster, playwright, communications professional, and entrepreneur. Alex, who is currently an Associate Professor of political science, is a well-known academic with special interests in Caribbean identities, political cultures, and institutions.

Alex earned a Bachelor's Degree in Philosophy with a minor in Theatre, and a Master's Degree in Political Science from Florida Atlantic University (FAU). He completed a second Master's Degree in International Relations (Studies) with a focus on Global Institutions at Florida International University's (FIU). The thesis for the second MA: International Financial Institutions and Caribbean Development: A Comparison of Haiti & Jamaica, examines and discusses the impact of International Monetary Fund (IMF) and World Bank (WB) policies on the United Nations Development Program (UNDP) measurements in Haiti and Jamaica.

The thesis explained the difficulties of those nations attaining the United Nation's Millennium Development Goals (MDGs). This ties into Bruno's interest in studying the Caribbean region in line with the identities of the peoples of the Caribbean. Alex presented a public lecture on his research, Calypso & Soca: the Journey of Two Musical Genres in Dominic, at the University of the West Indies, Open Campus – Dominica, on February 14, 2014. He also lectured on his research findings as follows: Mandela, Marley, Garvey and King: Four Different Voices, One Main Cause: Philosophical Concepts of Equal Rights which transcends all Boarders; at Florida Atlantic University in 2014, and the Concept of the American Dream: its epistemology and propensity for continuance as a metaphor for the unique American sovereign principle. The latter was presented on September 13, 2011 at Florida Atlantic University's House Chambers in Boca Raton, Florida. Bruno also researched and presented a public Lecture on - The Philosophy of Livity and the Key to Longevity: The Dominican Centenarian Perspective. The presentation was given at the University of the West Indies (Dominica Open Campus) on November 5 -7, 2009.

Also By Alex Bruno

The word 'kaiso' is an acclamation, like Bravo! Rooted in African customs, the word was used to express satisfaction about powerful expression of literary and performing art. The Caribbean is the birthplace of Calypso.
In fact, since Calypso landed on the West, following the atrocious journey of enslaved Africans across the Atlantic, it has been one of the most potent forms of expressions.
This book is meant to introduce kaiso to the a generation Caribbean and global citizens.

https://www.amazon.com/author/booksbyalex

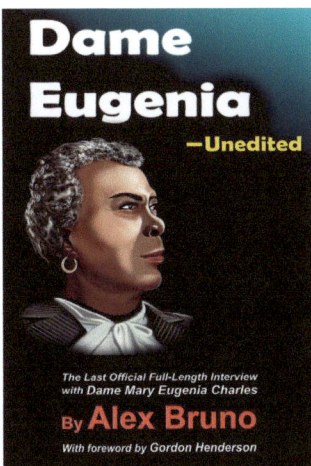

A frank and free-flowing discussion with one of the Caribbean's most recognizable political figures, Dame Mary Eugenia Charles of Dominica. What was certainly my most compelling media moment is now a treasure to the world of political leadership, and a welcome addition to Dominica's political history. Read through the text as you listen to the commanding voice of the Dame in this last full-length interview with the Caribbean's Iron Lady.

https://www.amazon.com/author/booksbyalex

Special Thanks To

Mr. & Mrs. Bernard Sylvester for sponsoring the artwork for this book your support is greatly appreciated.

www.ingramcontent.com/pod-product-compliance
Lightning Source LLC
Chambersburg PA
CBHW041555040426
42447CB00002B/180